JUST **3** STEPS

JUST **3** STEPS

Love Food ® is an imprint of
Parragon Books Ltd

Parragon
Queen Street House
4 Queen Street
Bath BA1 1HE, UK

Design: Terry Jeavons & Company
Additional photography: Clive Bozzard-Hill
Home economists: Valerie Barrett and
Carol Tennant
Introduction and additional recipes:
Christine McFadden

ISBN 978-1-4075-3390-2

Printed in China

This book uses imperial, metric, and U.S.
cup measurements. Follow the same units
of measurement throughout; do not mix
imperial and metric. All spoon measurements
are level, unless otherwise stated: teaspoons
are assumed to be 5ml, and tablespoons
are assumed to be 15ml. Unless otherwise
stated, milk is assumed to be whole, eggs
and individual fruits, such as bananas, are
medium, and pepper is freshly ground
black pepper.

Recipes using raw or very lightly cooked eggs
should be avoided by children, the elderly,
pregnant women, convalescents, and anyone
with an illness. Pregnant and breast-feeding
women are advised to avoid eating peanuts
and peanut products.

Contents

Introduction

If you don't always have the time or inclination to cook but love good food, this is the book for you. From start to finish, every recipe can be made in just three simple steps, whether it's a midweek meal, a special-occasion dinner, a solitary supper, or a feast for friends.

There are no long lists of ingredients or elaborate instructions to overwhelm you and the recipes are clear and concise, and written in a logical step-by-step order. The ingredients lists are laid out in an easy-to-read format, are broken down into smaller sections where necessary, and can be used as a checklist for the pantry or a trip to the stores. Some of the ingredients need simple advance preparation, but once that's out of the way the recipes couldn't be simpler. Even the more time-consuming recipes can be made in only three steps and are just as quick to prepare and as hassle free as the speedier dishes—many can be left to marinate or simmer away for an hour or two while you do something more interesting.

It's a good idea to spend a little time getting organized before you start cooking to make meal preparation even easier.

- Read the recipe all the way through, making a note of any soaking, chilling, or marinating stages.

- Assemble the pans and utensils you're going to need—that way you won't be frantically looking for something when the dish you're cooking needs urgent attention.

- Gather together all the ingredients before you start to cook.

- Make sure your knives are sharp. Get in the habit of passing the blade over a sharpener each time you use it, so you can chop and slice cleanly and quickly.

- Clean up as you go along.

With your utensils and ingredients assembled, you can relax and enjoy the actual process of easy three-step cooking. You'll be amazed by the sheer variety of dishes that can be produced this way—from tasty salads and soups to impressive meat, poultry, or fish main courses. There are inspiring dishes for vegetarians that are sure to tempt most palates, and also a chapter devoted to fabulous desserts.

1 Light Bites

If you're short of time and need something
simple to eat, these recipes are the answer.
They show you how to rustle up a variety of
mouthwatering but quickly prepared dishes
in just three steps. From sustaining soups
to substantial salads, and from pizzas and
bruschetta to sandwiches and wraps, these
tasty light meals and snacks will keep you
going at any time of day or night.

Chunky Vegetable Soup

INGREDIENTS

2 carrots, sliced

1 onion, diced

1 garlic clove, crushed

12 oz/350 g new potatoes, diced

2 celery stalks, sliced

4 oz/115 g button mushrooms, quartered

14 oz/400 g canned chopped tomatoes

2½ cups vegetable stock

1 bay leaf

1 tsp dried mixed herbs

½ cup corn kernels, frozen or canned, drained

2 oz/55 g green cabbage, shredded

pepper

serves 6

1 Put the carrots, onion, garlic, potatoes, celery, mushrooms, tomatoes, and stock into a large pan. Stir in the bay leaf and herbs. Bring to a boil, then reduce the heat, cover, and let simmer for 25 minutes.

2 Add the corn and cabbage and return to a boil. Reduce the heat, cover, and let simmer for 5 minutes, or until the vegetables are tender. Remove and discard the bay leaf. Season to taste with pepper.

3 Ladle into warmed bowls and serve immediately.

Leek & Potato Soup

INGREDIENTS

¼ cup butter

1 onion, chopped

3 leeks, sliced

8 oz/225 g potatoes, cut into
¾-inch/2-cm cubes

3½ cups vegetable stock

⅔ cup light cream (optional)

salt and pepper

fresh flat-leaf parsley
sprigs, to garnish

crusty bread, to serve

serves **4** to **6**

1 Melt the butter in a large saucepan over medium heat, add the onion, leeks, and potatoes, and sauté gently for 2–3 minutes, until softened but not browned. Pour in the stock, bring to a boil, then reduce the heat and simmer, covered, for 15 minutes.

2 Transfer the mixture to a food processor or blender and process until smooth. Return to the rinsed-out saucepan.

3 Reheat the soup, season to taste with salt and pepper, and serve in warmed bowls. Swirl with the cream, if using, garnish with parsley, and serve with crusty bread.

Chicken Noodle Soup

INGREDIENTS

2 skinless, boneless chicken breasts

5 cups water or chicken stock

3 carrots, cut into ¼-inch/ 5-mm slices

3 oz/85 g vermicelli (or other small noodles)

salt and pepper

fresh tarragon leaves, to garnish

serves ❹ to ❻

1 Place the chicken in a large saucepan, add the water, and bring to a simmer. Cook for 25–30 minutes. Skim any foam from the surface if necessary. Remove the chicken from the stock and keep warm.

2 Continue to simmer the liquid, add the carrots and vermicelli, and cook for 4–5 minutes.

3 Thinly slice or shred the chicken and place in warmed serving dishes. Season the soup to taste with salt and pepper and pour over the chicken. Garnish with tarragon and serve immediately.

Pear & Roquefort Open Sandwiches

INGREDIENTS

serves **2**

4 slices walnut bread, about ½ inch/1 cm thick

4 thin slices cured ham, such as Bayonne or prosciutto

2 ripe pears, halved, cored, and thinly sliced lengthwise

3½ oz/100 g Roquefort cheese, very thinly sliced

1 Preheat the broiler to high. Put the bread slices under the broiler and toast until crisp, but not browned, on both sides. Do not turn off the broiler.

2 Fold or cut the ham slices to cover each slice of bread, then divide the pear slices equally among them. Lay the cheese slices on top.

3 Return the open sandwiches to the broiler until the cheese melts and bubbles. Serve immediately.

Mushroom Fajitas

INGREDIENTS

serves **4**

2 tbsp oil

1 lb 2 oz/500 g portobello mushrooms, sliced

1 onion, sliced

1 red bell pepper, seeded and sliced

1 green bell pepper, seeded and sliced

1 garlic clove, crushed

¼–½ tsp cayenne pepper

juice and grated rind of 2 limes

2 tsp sugar

1 tsp dried oregano

8 flour tortillas

salt and pepper

salsa and lime wedges, to serve

1 Heat the oil in a large heavy-bottom skillet. Add the mushrooms, onion, red and green bell peppers, and garlic, and stir-fry for 8–10 minutes, until the vegetables are cooked.

2 Add the cayenne pepper, lime juice, lime rind, sugar, and oregano. Season to taste with salt and pepper and cook for an additional 2 minutes.

3 Meanwhile, heat the tortillas according to the package instructions. Divide the mushroom mixture among the warmed tortillas, roll up, and serve with salsa and lime wedges.

Nachos

INGREDIENTS

6 oz/175 g tortilla chips

14 oz/400 g canned refried beans, warmed

2 tbsp finely chopped bottled jalapeño chiles

7 oz/200 g canned or bottled pimientos or roasted bell peppers, drained and finely sliced

1 cup grated Gruyère cheese

1 cup grated cheddar cheese

salt and pepper

guacamole and sour cream, to serve

serves ❻

1 Preheat the oven to 400°F/200°C. Spread the tortilla chips out over the bottom of a large, shallow ovenproof dish or roasting pan.

2 Cover the tortilla chips with the warmed refried beans. Sprinkle over the chiles and pimientos and season to taste with salt and pepper. Mix the cheeses together in a bowl and sprinkle on top.

3 Bake in the preheated oven for 5–8 minutes, until the cheese is bubbling and melted. Serve immediately with guacamole and sour cream.

Brunch Bruschetta

INGREDIENTS

4 slices ciabatta bread

1 large ripe tomato, diced

2 scallions, finely sliced

1 small fresh buffalo mozzarella cheese, diced

½ ripe avocado, diced

½ tbsp balsamic vinegar

2 tbsp extra virgin olive oil

salt and pepper

2 tbsp shredded fresh basil leaves, to garnish

serves ❷

1 Preheat the broiler to medium–high. Place the ciabatta on a piece of foil on the rack in the broiler pan. Toast until lightly browned, then turn and cook on the other side. Reserve and keep warm.

2 Mix the tomato, scallions, mozzarella cheese, avocado, balsamic vinegar, and half of the oil together in a medium bowl. Season to taste with salt and pepper.

3 Drizzle the remaining oil over the ciabatta toast and top with the tomato mixture. Garnish with basil and serve immediately.

Miniature Ham & Pineapple Pizzas

INGREDIENTS

serves ❹

4 English muffins

½ cup prepared tomato pizza sauce

2 sun-dried tomatoes in oil, drained and chopped

2 oz/55 g Parma ham

2 rings canned pineapple, chopped

½ green bell pepper, seeded and chopped

4½ oz/125 g mozzarella cheese, cubed

olive oil, for drizzling

salt and pepper

1 Preheat the broiler to medium. Cut the English muffins in half and toast the cut side lightly under the preheated broiler.

2 Spread the tomato sauce evenly over the English muffins. Sprinkle the sun-dried tomatoes on top of the tomato sauce. Cut the Parma ham into thin strips and place on the English muffins with the pineapple and bell pepper. Carefully arrange the mozzarella cubes on top.

3 Drizzle a little oil over each pizza and season to taste with salt and pepper. Place under the preheated broiler and cook until the cheese melts and bubbles. Serve immediately.

Chorizo & Cheese Quesadillas

INGREDIENTS

serves 4

1 cup grated mozzarella cheese

1 cup grated cheddar cheese

8 oz/225 g cooked chorizo sausage (outer casing removed), diced

4 scallions, finely chopped

2 green chiles, seeded and finely chopped

8 flour tortillas

vegetable oil, for brushing

salt and pepper

guacamole and salsa, to serve

1 Place the cheeses, chorizo, scallions, chiles, and salt and pepper to taste in a bowl and mix together. Divide the mixture among 4 of the flour tortillas, then top with the remaining tortillas.

2 Brush a large nonstick or heavy-bottom skillet with oil and heat over medium heat. Add 1 quesadilla and cook, pressing it down with a spatula, for 4–5 minutes, until the underside is crisp and lightly browned. Turn over and cook the other side until the cheese is melting. Remove from the skillet and keep warm. Cook the remaining quesadillas.

3 Cut each quesadilla into quarters, arrange on a warmed serving plate, and serve with guacamole and salsa.

Chicken Wraps

INGREDIENTS

serves **4**

⅔ cup plain yogurt

1 tbsp whole-grain mustard

10 oz/280 g cooked skinless, boneless chicken breast, diced

5 oz/140 g iceberg lettuce, finely shredded

3 oz/85 g cucumber, thinly sliced

2 celery stalks, sliced

½ cup black seedless grapes, halved

8 flour tortillas

pepper

1 Combine the yogurt and mustard in a bowl and season to taste with pepper. Stir in the chicken and toss until thoroughly coated.

2 Put the lettuce, cucumber, celery, and grapes into a separate bowl and mix well.

3 Fold a tortilla in half and in half again to make a cone that is easy to hold. Half-fill the tortilla pocket with the salad mixture and top with some of the chicken mixture. Repeat with the remaining tortillas, salad, and chicken. Serve immediately.

Raisin Coleslaw & Tuna-Filled Pita Breads

INGREDIENTS

serves 4

scant ½ cup grated carrot

2 oz/55 g white cabbage, thinly sliced

⅓ cup plain yogurt

1 tsp cider vinegar

2 tbsp raisins

7 oz/200 g canned tuna steak in water, drained

2 tbsp pumpkin seeds

4 pita breads

pepper

4 apples, to serve

1 Mix the carrot, cabbage, yogurt, vinegar, and raisins together in a bowl. Lightly stir in the tuna and half the pumpkin seeds and season to taste with pepper.

2 Lightly toast the pita breads under a preheated hot broiler or in a toaster, then let cool slightly. Using a sharp knife, cut each pita bread in half.

2 Divide the filling evenly among the pita breads. Core the apples and cut into wedges, then serve immediately with the filled pita breads.

Greek Salad

INGREDIENTS

4 tomatoes, cut into wedges

1 onion, sliced

½ cucumber, sliced

1⅓ cups olives, pitted

8 oz/225 g feta cheese, cubed
(drained weight)

2 tbsp fresh cilantro leaves

fresh flat-leaf parsley
sprigs, to garnish

pita bread, to serve

DRESSING

5 tbsp extra virgin olive oil

2 tbsp white wine vinegar

1 tbsp lemon juice

½ tsp sugar

1 tbsp chopped fresh
cilantro

salt and pepper

serves ❹

1 To make the dressing, place the oil, vinegar, lemon juice, sugar, and cilantro in a large bowl. Season to taste with salt and pepper and mix together well.

2 Place the tomatoes, onion, cucumber, olives, feta cheese, and cilantro in a bowl and pour over the dressing.

3 Toss all the ingredients together, then divide among individual serving bowls. Garnish with parsley sprigs and serve with pita bread.

Roasted Vegetable Salad

INGREDIENTS

serves 4

1 onion

1 eggplant

1 red bell pepper, seeded

1 orange bell pepper, seeded

1 large zucchini

2–4 garlic cloves

2–4 tbsp olive oil

1 tbsp balsamic vinegar

2 tbsp extra virgin olive oil

1 tbsp shredded fresh basil

salt and pepper

Parmesan cheese shavings, to serve

1 Preheat the oven to 400°F/200°C. Cut all the vegetables into even-size wedges, put into a roasting pan, and scatter over the garlic. Pour over 2 tablespoons of the olive oil and toss the vegetables until well coated with the oil. Season to taste with salt and pepper. Roast in the preheated oven for 40 minutes, or until tender, adding more olive oil if needed.

2 Meanwhile, put the vinegar, extra virgin olive oil, and salt and pepper to taste into a screw-top jar and shake until blended.

3 Once the vegetables are cooked, remove from the oven, arrange on a serving dish, and pour over the dressing. Sprinkle with the basil and serve with Parmesan cheese shavings.

Steak Waldorf Salad

INGREDIENTS

serves 4

2 tenderloin steaks, about 6 oz/175 g each and 1 inch/ 2.5 cm thick

olive or corn oil, for brushing

1 tbsp whole-grain mustard

⅔ cup mayonnaise

1 tbsp lemon juice

1 lb 2 oz/500 g apples

4 celery stalks, thinly sliced

½ cup walnut halves, broken into pieces

3½ oz/100 g mixed salad greens

pepper

crusty bread, to serve

1 Heat a cast-iron grill pan or heavy-bottom skillet over medium heat. Brush each steak with oil and season to taste with pepper. Add the steaks to the pan and cook for 6–7 minutes for rare or 8–10 minutes for medium, turning the steaks frequently and brushing once or twice with oil. Remove from the pan and set aside.

2 Meanwhile, stir the mustard into the mayonnaise. Put the lemon juice into a large bowl. Peel and core the apples, then cut them into small chunks and immediately toss in the lemon juice. Stir in the mustard mayonnaise. Add the celery and walnuts to the apple mixture and toss together.

3 Arrange the salad greens on 4 plates, then divide the apple mixture among them. Very thinly slice the steaks, arrange on top of the salads, and serve immediately with crusty bread.

Smoked Salmon, Asparagus & Avocado Salad

INGREDIENTS

serves ④

7 oz/200 g fresh asparagus spears

1 large ripe avocado

1 tbsp lemon juice

large handful fresh arugula leaves

8 oz/225 g smoked salmon

1 red onion, finely sliced

1 tbsp chopped fresh parsley

1 tbsp snipped fresh chives

salt

DRESSING

1 garlic clove, chopped

4 tbsp extra virgin olive oil

2 tbsp white wine vinegar

1 tbsp lemon juice

pinch of sugar

1 tsp mustard

1 Bring a large pan of salted water to a boil. Add the asparagus and cook for 4 minutes, then drain. Refresh under cold running water and drain again. Set aside to cool.

2 To make the dressing, combine all the ingredients in a small bowl and stir together well. Cut the avocado in half lengthwise, then remove and discard the pit and skin. Cut the flesh into bite-size pieces and brush with lemon juice to prevent discoloration.

3 To assemble the salad, arrange the arugula on individual serving plates and top with the asparagus and avocado. Cut the smoked salmon into strips and scatter over the top of the salad, then scatter over the onion and herbs. Drizzle over the dressing and serve.

2 Meat

With its appetizing flavor and texture, meat is an all-time favorite. Take your pick from richly flavored beef, sweet and delicate lamb, or tasty pork and ham. There is a wonderful choice of cooking methods that will bring out the best in the meat you have bought. The recipes include speedy stir-fries and broils, succulent roasts, comforting meat loaf, and pasta dishes, as well as leisurely stews and casseroles that take care of themselves while cooking.

Broiled Steak with Tomatoes & Garlic

INGREDIENTS

3 tbsp olive oil, plus extra
for brushing

1 lb 9 oz/700 g tomatoes,
peeled and chopped

1 red bell pepper, seeded
and chopped

1 onion, chopped

2 garlic cloves, finely
chopped

1 tbsp chopped fresh
flat-leaf parsley

1 tsp dried oregano

1 tsp sugar

4 entrecôte steaks or rump
steaks, about 6 oz/175 g each

salt and pepper

cooked green beans and
new potatoes, to serve

serves 4

1 Place the oil, tomatoes, red bell pepper,
onion, garlic, parsley, oregano, and sugar in a
heavy-bottom saucepan and season to taste
with salt and pepper. Bring to a boil, reduce
the heat, and simmer for 15 minutes.

2 Meanwhile, preheat the broiler to high or
preheat a grill pan over high heat. Snip any fat
around the outsides of the steaks. Season each
generously with pepper and brush with oil.
Cook for 1 minute on each side, then reduce the
heat to medium and cook according to taste:
1½–2 minutes each side for rare; 2½–3 minutes
each side for medium; 3–4 minutes on each side
for well done.

3 Transfer the steaks to warmed individual
plates with the sauce. Serve immediately with
green beans and new potatoes.

The Best Burgers

INGREDIENTS

1 lb 2 oz/500 g ground steak

½ small onion, very finely chopped or grated (optional)

vegetable oil, for brushing

salt and pepper

TO SERVE

4 hamburger buns

lettuce leaves

sliced gherkins (optional)

tomato relish or other sauce of your choice

serves ❹

1 Preheat the broiler to medium–high. Place the ground steak in a bowl, add the onion, if using, and season to taste with salt and pepper. Mix well together, divide into 4 portions, and shape each into a round patty, about 1 inch/ 2.5 cm thick.

2 Brush the burgers with oil and cook under the preheated broiler, turning once, for 8–12 minutes, until browned and cooked through.

3 Meanwhile, split the hamburger buns in half and place the lettuce leaves on the bottom halves. Put a cooked burger on top of each and add the gherkins, if using, and tomato relish. Top with the remaining hamburger bun halves and serve immediately.

Beef & Pearl Onion Casserole

INGREDIENTS

serves 6

2 tbsp olive oil

1 lb/450 g pearl onions,
peeled but kept whole

2 garlic cloves, halved

2 lb/900 g braising beef, cubed

½ tsp ground cinnamon

1 tsp ground cloves

1 tsp ground cumin

2 tbsp tomato paste

3 cups red wine

grated rind and juice of
1 orange

1 bay leaf

salt and pepper

1 tbsp chopped fresh
flat-leaf parsley, to garnish

mashed potatoes, to serve

1 Preheat the oven to 300°F/150°C. Heat the oil in a large flameproof casserole and cook the whole onions and garlic, stirring frequently, for 5 minutes, or until softened and beginning to brown. Add the beef and cook over high heat, stirring frequently, for 5 minutes, or until browned on all sides.

2 Stir the spices and tomato paste into the casserole and season to taste with salt and pepper. Pour in the wine, scraping any sediment from the bottom of the casserole, then add the orange rind, orange juice, and bay leaf. Bring to a boil and cover.

3 Cook in the preheated oven for about 2 hours. Remove the lid and cook the casserole for an additional hour, stirring once or twice, until the meat is tender. Remove from the oven, garnish with parsley, and serve hot with mashed potatoes.

Beef & Red Wine Pot Roast

INGREDIENTS

3 lb 8 oz–4 lb /1.6 kg–1.8 kg rolled beef round or brisket

3 tbsp vegetable oil

1 onion, finely chopped

2 celery stalks, finely diced

2 carrots, finely diced

1 fresh bay leaf

1 heaping tsp dried thyme

⅔ cup meat stock

1¼–1½ cups red wine

½ tbsp all-purpose flour, plus extra for dusting

salt and pepper

serves ❻

1 Preheat the oven to 300°F/150°C. Season the meat well with salt and pepper and dust with flour. Heat the oil in a flameproof casserole in which the meat fits snugly. Cook the meat on all sides until browned and transfer to a plate. Add the onion, celery, and carrots to the casserole and cook until softened.

2 Return the meat to the casserole, add the bay leaf, thyme, stock, and enough wine to come one-third of the way up the meat. Bring to a boil, cover tightly with a lid, and put in the preheated oven. Cook for 3–3½ hours, turning occasionally and topping up the liquid, if necessary. Transfer the meat to a warmed serving platter and cover loosely with foil.

3 Using paper towels, remove any excess fat from the surface of the liquid in the casserole. Strain the remaining liquid into a saucepan and bring to a boil, adding any juices from the meat. Mix the flour to a thin paste with a little water and whisk into the liquid to thicken. Check the seasoning and adjust, if necessary. Pour a little of the sauce over the meat and serve the remainder in a pitcher.

Hot & Spicy Beef with Toasted Pine Nuts

INGREDIENTS

serves ❹

3 tbsp soy sauce

1½ tbsp cornstarch

1 lb/450 g rump steak

2 oz/55 g pine nuts

juice of 1 lime

2 tbsp white wine vinegar

2 tbsp peanut oil

3 tsp grated fresh ginger

2 red chiles, finely chopped

4 baby leeks, halved

2 carrots, thinly sliced

3½ oz/100 g fine tip asparagus

3 shallots, thinly sliced

cooked noodles, to serve

1 Mix 2 tablespoons of the soy sauce with 1 tablespoon of the cornstarch and 1 tablespoon of cold water in a medium bowl. Cut the beef into thin strips, then add to the bowl and stir until the meat is well coated. Cover with plastic wrap and let chill in the refrigerator for 1 hour. Meanwhile, preheat the broiler to medium. Spread the pine nuts on a baking sheet and toast under the preheated broiler. Set aside.

2 Mix the lime juice, vinegar, the remaining cornstarch, the remaining soy sauce, and 1 tablespoon of the oil in a small bowl and set aside. Heat the remaining oil in a large skillet or wok. Stir-fry the ginger, chiles, and leeks for 2 minutes. Add the beef mixture and stir-fry for an additional minute.

3 Stir in the carrots, asparagus, and shallots and stir-fry for 7 minutes, or until the beef is cooked through. Add the lime mixture, reduce the heat, and simmer until the liquid thickens. Remove from the heat, sprinkle with the reserved pine nuts, and serve with cooked noodles.

Meatloaf

INGREDIENTS

1 thick slice white bread, crusts removed

3 cups ground beef, pork, or lamb

1 small egg

1 tbsp finely chopped onion

1 beef bouillon cube, crumbled

1 tsp dried mixed herbs

salt and pepper

TO SERVE

sauce or gravy

mashed potatoes

cooked string beans

serves ❹

1 Preheat the oven to 350°F/180°C. Put the bread into a small bowl and add enough water to soak. Let stand for 5 minutes, then drain and squeeze well to remove the water. Crumble the bread into small pieces.

2 Combine the bread with the meat, egg, onion, bouillon cube, and herbs in a bowl and season to taste with salt and pepper. Shape into a loaf, then place on a baking sheet or in an ovenproof dish.

3 Bake the meatloaf in the preheated oven for 30–45 minutes, until the juices run clear when it is pierced with a skewer. Cut into slices and serve with sauce, mashed potatoes, and string beans.

Lamb Chops with Mint

INGREDIENTS

serves ❹

**6 lamb chump chops, about
6 oz/175 g each**

⅔ cup strained plain yogurt

**2 garlic cloves, finely
chopped**

1 tsp grated fresh ginger

**¼ tsp coriander seeds,
crushed**

**1 tbsp olive oil, plus extra
for brushing**

1 tbsp orange juice

1 tsp walnut oil

2 tbsp chopped fresh mint

salt and pepper

1 Place the chops in a large, shallow nonmetallic bowl. Mix half the yogurt, the garlic, ginger, and coriander seeds together in a measuring cup and season to taste with salt and pepper. Spoon the mixture over the chops, turning to coat, then cover with plastic wrap and let marinate in the refrigerator for 2 hours, turning occasionally.

2 Preheat the barbecue or broiler. Place the remaining yogurt, the olive oil, orange juice, walnut oil, and mint in a small bowl and whisk until thoroughly blended. Season to taste with salt and pepper. Cover with plastic wrap and let chill in the refrigerator until ready to serve.

3 Drain the chops, scraping off the marinade. Brush with olive oil and cook over medium–hot coals or under the preheated broiler for 5–7 minutes on each side. Serve immediately with the minted yogurt.

Lamb Tagine

INGREDIENTS

12 oz/350 g boneless lamb

1 tbsp sunflower oil

1 onion, chopped

1 garlic clove, finely chopped

2½ cups vegetable stock

grated rind and juice of
1 orange

1 tsp clear honey

1 cinnamon stick

½-inch/1-cm piece fresh
ginger, finely chopped

1 eggplant

4 tomatoes, peeled and
chopped

⅔ cup plumped dried apricots

2 tbsp chopped fresh
cilantro

salt and pepper

cooked couscous, to serve

serves 4

1 Trim all visible fat from the lamb and cut into 1-inch/2.5-cm cubes. Heat the oil in a large heavy-bottom skillet or flameproof casserole over medium heat. Add the onion and lamb and cook, stirring frequently, for 5 minutes, or until the meat is lightly browned all over. Add the garlic, stock, orange rind, orange juice, honey, cinnamon stick, and ginger. Bring to a boil, then reduce the heat, cover, and simmer for 45 minutes.

2 Using a sharp knife, halve the eggplant lengthwise and slice thinly. Add to the skillet with the tomatoes and apricots. Cover and cook for an additional 45 minutes, or until the lamb is tender.

3 Stir in the cilantro and season to taste with salt and pepper. Serve immediately with cooked couscous.

Caramelized Lamb Shanks with Root Vegetables

INGREDIENTS

serves 4

4 tbsp clear honey

1 tbsp vegetable oil

1 tsp dried thyme or oregano

2 tsp pepper

½ tsp salt

4 lamb shanks, about 14 oz/ 400 g each

1½–2 cups stock

1 head garlic, unpeeled, sliced in half across the center

1 onion, quartered

1 parsnip, quartered lengthwise

4 small new potatoes, halved lengthwise

4 small carrots

1 Preheat the oven to 350°F/180°C. Mix together the honey, oil, thyme, pepper, and salt, and rub all over the lamb shanks. Put the lamb shanks in a roasting pan with ¾ cup of the stock, the garlic, and onion.

2 Cook in the preheated oven for 1 hour, turning the lamb after 30 minutes. Turn again, and add the parsnip, potatoes, carrots, and ⅔ cup of the remaining stock. Cook for an additional 30 minutes and turn the lamb again. Add a little more stock, if necessary, then cook for an additional 15 minutes.

3 Using a slotted spoon, transfer the meat and vegetables to a warmed serving dish. Using paper towels, remove any excess fat from the surface of the liquid in the pan. Place the pan over medium heat and stir for a few seconds, until the liquid is syrupy. Pour over the meat and vegetables, and serve immediately.

Glazed Ham Steaks

INGREDIENTS

4 ham steaks

4 tbsp brown sugar

2 tsp mustard powder

4 tbsp butter

8 rings canned pineapple

serves ❹

1 Preheat a grill pan over medium heat. Place the ham steaks in it and cook for 5 minutes, turning once. If you only have room for 2 steaks at a time, cook them completely and keep them warm while cooking the second pair.

2 Combine the brown sugar and mustard in a small bowl. Melt the butter in a large skillet. Add the pineapple and cook for 2 minutes to heat through, turning once. Sprinkle with the sugar and mustard mixture and continue cooking over low heat until the sugar has melted and the pineapple is well glazed. Turn the pineapple once more, so that both sides are coated with sauce.

3 Place the ham steaks on individual plates and top each with 2 pineapple rings. Spoon over the pan juices and serve.

Pork Chops with Rosemary & White Beans

INGREDIENTS

2 thick pork loin chops, about 10½–12 oz/300–350 g each

olive oil, for brushing

generous pat of butter

1 garlic clove, crushed

1 tsp finely chopped fresh rosemary, plus extra sprigs to garnish

14 oz/400 g canned cannellini beans, drained and rinsed

salt and pepper

serves ❷

1 Season the pork chops well with salt and pepper and brush with oil. Heat a nonstick heavy-bottom saucepan over medium heat. Cook the chops for 5 minutes on each side, until browned. Reduce the heat, cover the pan, and cook for an additional 10–15 minutes, depending on thickness, turning once.

2 Meanwhile, heat the butter with the garlic and chopped rosemary in a small saucepan over medium heat. Add all but 3 tablespoons of the beans and moisten with 2 tablespoons of water. Stir to heat through, then mash to a coarse puree with the back of a wooden spoon. Season to taste with salt and pepper.

3 Divide the mashed beans between 2 warmed plates. Top each with a pork chop and pour over the pan juices. Briefly warm the reserved whole beans, then scatter over the chops. Garnish with rosemary sprigs and serve.

Roasted Fennel Pork Tenderloin

INGREDIENTS

serves ❷ to ❸

1 pork tenderloin, about 1 lb 4 oz–1 lb 5 oz/550–600 g

3 tbsp olive oil

1½ tsp fennel seeds

1 large garlic clove

1½ tsp finely chopped fresh rosemary

¾ tsp sea salt

¾ tsp pepper

2 tsp balsamic vinegar

2 fennel bulbs, trimmed and very thinly sliced

½ cup stock

1 Make slits all over the meat with a sharp knife. Rub with 1 tablespoon of the oil. In a mortar, grind the fennel seeds, garlic, rosemary, salt, and pepper to a coarse paste with a pestle. Push about two-thirds into the slits in the pork. Mix together the vinegar, the remaining oil, and the remaining paste in a bowl, add the fennel, and toss to mix. Let marinate for 30 minutes.

2 Preheat the oven to 425°F/220°C. Place the pork and fennel in a shallow roasting pan, add the stock, and cook in the preheated oven for 10 minutes. Reduce the heat to 375°F/190°C and roast for an additional 10–15 minutes, stirring occasionally.

3 Transfer the pork to a warmed serving dish, cover loosely with foil, and let rest for 15 minutes in a warm place. Meanwhile, return the roasting pan with the fennel to the switched-off oven. Carve the meat into thick diagonal slices, then top with the fennel and any juices from the pan and serve.

Spaghetti alla Carbonara

INGREDIENTS

1 lb/450 g dried spaghetti

1 tbsp olive oil

8 oz/225 g rindless pancetta
or bacon, chopped

4 eggs

5 tbsp light cream

2 tbsp freshly grated
Parmesan cheese

salt and pepper

serves ❹

1 Bring a large heavy-bottom pan of lightly salted water to a boil. Add the pasta, return to a boil, and cook for 8–10 minutes, or until tender but still firm to the bite.

2 Meanwhile, heat the oil in a heavy-bottom skillet. Add the pancetta and cook over medium heat, stirring frequently, for 8–10 minutes.

3 Beat the eggs with the cream in a small bowl and season to taste with salt and pepper. Drain the pasta and return it to the pan. Turn in the contents of the skillet, then add the egg mixture and half the Parmesan cheese. Stir well, then transfer to a warmed serving dish. Serve immediately, sprinkled with the remaining cheese.

3 Poultry

Whether it's a simple roast chicken, a juicy pan-fried duck breast, or a spicy turkey stir-fry, poultry is one of the most good-tempered and versatile foods. It combines perfectly with a wide spectrum of tasty ingredients, offering endless inspiration for delicious meals. As the recipes in this chapter show, you can create curries and casseroles, roasts and stir-fries, or burgers and broils in just three easy steps.

Chicken Pepperonata

INGREDIENTS

serves 4

8 skinless chicken thighs

2 tbsp whole-wheat flour

2 tbsp olive oil

1 small onion, thinly sliced

1 garlic clove, crushed

1 each large red, yellow, and green bell peppers, seeded and thinly sliced

14 oz/400 g canned chopped tomatoes

1 tbsp chopped fresh oregano, plus extra to garnish

salt and pepper

crusty whole-wheat bread, to serve

1 Toss the chicken thighs in the flour, shaking off the excess. Heat the oil in a wide skillet and cook the chicken quickly until sealed and lightly browned, then remove from the pan.

2 Add the onion to the skillet and cook gently until softened. Add the garlic, bell peppers, tomatoes, and oregano, then bring to a boil, stirring.

3 Arrange the chicken over the vegetables, season well with salt and pepper, then cover the skillet tightly and simmer for 20–25 minutes, or until the chicken is completely cooked and tender. Garnish with oregano and serve with crusty whole-wheat bread.

Tarragon Chicken

INGREDIENTS

serves **4**

4 skinless, boneless chicken breasts, about 6 oz/175 g each

½ cup dry white wine

1–1¼ cups chicken stock

1 garlic clove, finely chopped

1 tbsp dried tarragon

¾ cup heavy cream

1 tbsp chopped fresh tarragon

salt and pepper

cooked string beans, to serve

1 Season the chicken well with salt and pepper and place in a single layer in a large heavy-bottom skillet. Pour in the wine and enough chicken stock just to cover and add the garlic and dried tarragon. Bring to a boil, reduce the heat, and cook gently for 10 minutes, or until the chicken is tender and cooked through.

2 Remove the chicken with a slotted spoon, cover, and keep warm. Strain the poaching liquid into a clean skillet and skim off any fat from the surface. Bring to a boil and cook for 12–15 minutes, or until reduced by about two-thirds.

3 Stir in the cream, return to a boil, and cook until reduced by about half. Stir in the fresh tarragon. Arrange the chicken on warmed serving plates, spoon over the sauce, and serve immediately with cooked string beans.

Thai Red Chicken Curry

INGREDIENTS

6 garlic cloves, chopped

2 red chiles, chopped

2 tbsp chopped lemongrass

1 tsp finely grated lime rind

1 tbsp chopped lime leaves

1 tbsp Thai red curry paste

1 tbsp coriander seeds

1 tbsp chili oil

4 skinless, boneless chicken breasts, sliced

1¼ cups coconut milk

1¼ cups chicken stock

1 tbsp soy sauce

⅓ cup ground peanuts

3 scallions, diagonally sliced

1 red bell pepper, seeded and sliced

3 Thai eggplants, sliced

chopped fresh cilantro, to garnish

cooked rice, to serve

serves 2 to 4

1 Place the garlic, chiles, lemongrass, lime rind, lime leaves, curry paste, and coriander seeds in a food processor and process until the mixture is smooth.

2 Heat the oil in a preheated wok or large skillet over high heat. Add the chicken and garlic mixture and stir-fry for 5 minutes. Add the coconut milk, stock, and soy sauce and bring to a boil. Reduce the heat and cook, stirring, for an additional 3 minutes. Stir in the ground peanuts and simmer for 20 minutes.

3 Add the scallions, bell pepper, and eggplants and simmer, stirring occasionally, for an additional 10 minutes. Garnish with cilantro and serve with cooked rice.

Chicken Fried Rice

INGREDIENTS

½ tbsp sesame oil

6 shallots, quartered

1 lb/450 g cooked chicken, diced

3 tbsp soy sauce

2 carrots, diced

1 celery stalk, diced

1 red bell pepper, seeded and diced

1½ cups fresh peas

3½ oz/100 g canned corn kernels, drained

3⅔ cups cooked long-grain rice

2 large eggs, scrambled

serves 4

1 Heat the oil in a large skillet over medium heat. Add the shallots and cook until softened, then add the chicken and 2 tablespoons of the soy sauce and stir-fry for 5–6 minutes.

2 Stir in the carrots, celery, red bell pepper, peas, and corn and stir-fry for an additional 5 minutes. Add the rice and stir thoroughly.

3 Finally, stir in the scrambled eggs and the remaining soy sauce. Serve immediately.

Chicken Satay

INGREDIENTS

2 tbsp vegetable oil or peanut oil

1 tbsp sesame oil

juice of ½ lime

2 skinless, boneless chicken breasts, cut into small cubes

crushed peanuts, to garnish

DIP

2 tbsp vegetable oil or peanut oil

1 small onion, finely chopped

1 small green chile, seeded and chopped

1 garlic clove, finely chopped

½ cup crunchy peanut butter

6–8 tbsp water

juice of ½ lime

serves ❹

1 Combine both the oils and the lime juice in a nonmetallic dish. Add the chicken, cover with plastic wrap, and let chill for 1 hour.

2 To make the dip, heat the oil in a skillet and cook the onion, chile, and garlic over low heat, stirring occasionally, for about 5 minutes, until just softened. Add the peanut butter, water, and lime juice and let simmer gently, stirring constantly, until the peanut butter has softened enough to make a dip—you may need to add extra water to make a thinner consistency.

3 Preheat the barbecue or broiler. Drain the chicken cubes and thread them onto 8–12 presoaked wooden skewers. Cook over hot coals or under the preheated broiler, turning frequently, for about 10 minutes, until cooked and browned. Serve hot with the warm dip, garnished with crushed peanuts.

Paprika Chicken with Sour Cream

INGREDIENTS

serves **4**

1 tbsp butter

2 tbsp vegetable oil

1 onion, sliced

2 green bell peppers, seeded
and chopped

1 tbsp paprika

3 lb 5 oz/1.5 kg chicken
thighs and drumsticks

scant 1 cup stock

⅔ cup sour cream

1 tsp all-purpose flour

salt and pepper

1 tbsp snipped fresh dill,
to garnish

cooked rice, to serve

1 Heat the butter and 1 tablespoon of the oil in a
pan and cook the onion and green bell peppers
until softened. Stir in the paprika and season to
taste with salt and pepper. Cook for an additional
5 minutes, stirring occasionally.

2 Meanwhile, heat the remaining oil in a lidded
flameproof casserole dish or a heavy-bottom
saucepan and cook the chicken portions until
browned all over. Add the onion and bell pepper
mixture and the stock. Cover tightly and simmer
over low heat for 45 minutes. Remove the lid
and cook for an additional 15 minutes.

3 Remove the pan from the heat and remove any
excess fat from the surface with paper towels.
Return to medium–low heat, then gradually stir in
the sour cream and then the flour. Simmer gently
for 3–4 minutes, stirring, until thickened. Check
and adjust the seasoning, if necessary, sprinkle
with the dill, and serve with cooked rice.

Roast Chicken with Cumin Butter & Preserved Lemon

INGREDIENTS

½ scant cup butter, softened

½ tbsp cumin seeds, lightly crushed

½ preserved lemon, finely chopped

1 large garlic clove, crushed

1 whole chicken, about 3 lb 5 oz/1.5 kg

salt and pepper

roasted vegetables, to serve

serves ❸ to ❹

1 Preheat the oven to 425°F/220°C. Mash together the butter, cumin seeds, preserved lemon, and garlic, and season to taste with salt and pepper. Using your fingers, loosen the skin on the chicken breasts and legs. Push most of the flavored butter under the skin, molding it to the shape of the bird. Smear any remaining butter over the skin.

2 Place the chicken in a roasting pan and cook in the preheated oven for 20 minutes. Reduce the oven temperature to 350°F/180°C and cook for an additional 50–55 minutes, until the juices run clear when you pierce the thickest part of the chicken with a skewer. Transfer the chicken to a warmed serving dish, cover loosely with foil, and let rest for 15 minutes.

3 Pour off most of the fat from the roasting pan. Place the pan over medium heat and cook the juices for a few minutes, scraping any sediment from the bottom of the pan, until reduced slightly. Carve the chicken into slices, pour over the juice, and serve with roasted vegetables.

Turkey Scallops with Green Peppercorn Sauce

INGREDIENTS

serves **4**

1 tbsp vegetable oil

2 tbsp butter

2 shallots, chopped

1 lb 9 oz/700 g turkey scallops, cut into thin strips

8 oz/225 g button mushrooms, sliced

1¼ cups sour cream

1 tbsp green peppercorns in brine, drained

finely grated rind of ½ lemon

salt and pepper

snipped fresh chives, to garnish

1 Heat the oil and butter in a large heavy-bottom skillet, add the shallots, and cook until softened. Add the turkey and cook over medium–high heat until golden. Remove the turkey from the pan with a slotted spoon and keep warm.

2 Add the mushrooms to the pan and cook for 5 minutes, stirring, until softened. Return the turkey to the pan and season to taste with salt and pepper. Stir in the sour cream, peppercorns, and lemon rind, and warm through gently.

3 Transfer to a warmed serving dish, garnish with chives, and serve.

Lemon & Mint Turkey Burgers

INGREDIENTS

serves ❹

1 lb 2 oz/500 g ground turkey

½ small onion, grated

finely grated rind and juice
of 1 small lemon

1 garlic clove, finely chopped

2 tbsp finely chopped fresh
mint

½ tsp pepper

1 tsp sea salt

1 egg, beaten

1 tbsp olive oil, plus extra
for frying

lemon wedges, to serve

1 Place all the ingredients in a bowl and mix
well with a fork. Shape the mixture into
12 balls, rolling them with the palm of your
hand. Flatten into patties about ¾ inch/2 cm
thick. Cover and let chill in the refrigerator for
at least 1 hour, or overnight.

2 Heat about 5 tablespoons of oil in a large
heavy-bottom skillet. When the oil starts to
look hazy, add the burgers, cooking in batches
if necessary. Cook over medium–high heat for
4–5 minutes on each side, until browned and
cooked through.

3 Drain the burgers on paper towels and
transfer to a warmed serving dish. Serve with
lemon wedges.

Turkey & Cashew Nut Stir-Fry

INGREDIENTS

serves 4

1 tbsp cornstarch

½ tsp five-spice powder

4 turkey steaks, cut into thin strips

1 tsp soy sauce

1 tsp dry sherry

3 tbsp peanut oil

1 garlic clove, finely chopped

1-inch/2.5-cm piece fresh ginger, finely chopped

4 scallions, cut into thin strips

1 large carrot, cut into thin strips

⅔ cup cashew nuts

2 tbsp hoisin sauce

½ tsp salt

shredded scallions, to garnish

cooked rice, to serve

1 Mix together the cornstarch and five-spice powder in a bowl and stir in the turkey. Add the soy sauce and sherry, stirring to coat. Set aside for 30 minutes.

2 Heat a wok or large skillet over high heat. Heat 2 tablespoons of the oil, then add the turkey mixture and stir-fry for 2–3 minutes, until golden and cooked through. Using a slotted spoon, transfer the turkey to a plate and keep warm.

3 Heat the remaining oil in the wok and stir-fry the garlic, ginger, scallions, and carrot for 1 minute. Return the turkey to the wok with the cashew nuts, hoisin sauce, and salt. Reduce the heat to medium–high and stir-fry for an additional minute. Sprinkle with shredded scallions and serve immediately with cooked rice.

Balsamic-Glazed Duck Breasts

INGREDIENTS

serves 4

4 duck breasts with skin, about 7 oz/200 g each

4 tbsp stock

2 tbsp prepared balsamic vinegar glaze or balsamic vinegar

salt and pepper

cooked green beans and sautéed potatoes, to serve

1 Preheat the oven to 425°F/220°C. Slash the skin on each duck breast a few times and rub well with salt and pepper.

2 Heat an ovenproof skillet over medium–high heat. Cook the duck breasts skin-side down for 3–4 minutes. Transfer the skillet to the preheated oven and cook for an additional 5 minutes. Turn the duck breasts and cook for an additional 5 minutes. Transfer to a warmed serving dish and let rest for at least 10 minutes.

3 Pour off any excess fat from the skillet and stir in the stock over medium heat. Add the balsamic glaze and the juices from the duck. Simmer for a few seconds, until the liquid is syrupy. Cut the duck breasts into thick diagonal slices, pour over the sauce, and serve with cooked green beans and sautéed potatoes.

Roast Duck Legs with Pears & Ginger

INGREDIENTS

4 duck legs

2 firm pears, quartered, cored, and peeled

2 onions, quartered lengthwise

cooked noodles, to serve

MARINADE

1 tbsp grated fresh ginger

juice of 1 lemon

4 tbsp clear honey

2 tbsp soy sauce

2 tbsp toasted sesame oil

pepper

serves ❹

1 Combine the marinade ingredients in a shallow dish. Add the duck legs, toss in the marinade, and let marinate in the refrigerator for at least 2 hours, or overnight.

2 Preheat the oven to 350°F/180°C. Arrange the pear and onion quarters in the bottom of a small roasting pan with a rack. Pour in all but 4 tablespoons of the marinade. Place the duck legs on the rack and cook in the preheated oven for 40 minutes, brushing the duck with the reserved marinade. Turn over the duck and cook for an additional 15 minutes.

3 Transfer the duck legs, pears, and onions to a warmed serving dish. Drain off most of the fat from the pan. Place the pan over medium–high heat and briefly simmer the remaining liquid, stirring. Pour the sauce over the duck legs and serve with cooked noodles.

4 Fish & Seafood

Fish and seafood are so simple to cook that they are the perfect candidates for cooking in just three steps. Straightforward techniques make the most of their natural tenderness and clean, fresh flavors. Broiling, stir-frying, or shallow-frying, or just a quick roasting at a high temperature, are all that's needed to produce delectable results. Whatever cooking method you choose, make sure to use the freshest fish possible.

Salmon Steaks with Parsley Pesto

INGREDIENTS

4 salmon steaks, about 6 oz/175 g each

grilled lemon wedges, to garnish

fresh arugula, to serve

PARSLEY PESTO

2 garlic cloves, coarsely chopped

½ cup pine nuts

¾ cup fresh parsley leaves, coarse stems removed

1 tsp salt

⅓ cup freshly grated Parmesan cheese

½–⅔ cup extra virgin olive oil

serves ❹

1 To make the pesto, put the garlic, pine nuts, parsley, and salt into a food processor and blend to a puree. Add the Parmesan and blend briefly again. Add ½ cup oil and blend again. If the consistency is too thick, add the remaining oil and blend again until smooth. Scrape into a bowl and set aside.

2 Meanwhile, preheat the broiler to medium. Cook the salmon under the preheated broiler for 10–15 minutes, depending on the thickness of the fillets, until the flesh turns pink and flakes easily.

3 Transfer the salmon to individual serving plates. Garnish with lemon wedges and serve with the parsley pesto and arugula.

Salmon Sticks with Potato Wedges

INGREDIENTS

scant 1 cup fine cornmeal

1 tsp paprika

14 oz/400 g salmon fillet, skinned and sliced into 12 chunky sticks

1 egg, beaten

corn oil, for cooking

POTATO WEDGES

1 lb 2 oz/500 g potatoes, scrubbed and cut into thick wedges

1–2 tbsp olive oil

½ tsp paprika

salt

serves 2 to 3

1 Preheat the oven to 400°F/200°C. To make the potato wedges, dry the potatoes on a clean dish towel. Spoon the oil into a roasting pan and put into the preheated oven briefly to heat. Toss the potatoes in the warm oil until well coated. Sprinkle with paprika and salt to taste and roast for 30 minutes, turning halfway through, until crisp and golden.

2 Meanwhile, mix the cornmeal and paprika together on a plate. Dip each salmon stick into the beaten egg, then roll in the cornmeal mixture until evenly coated.

3 Heat enough oil to cover the bottom of a large heavy-bottom skillet over medium heat. Carefully arrange half the salmon sticks in the skillet and cook for 6 minutes, turning halfway through, until golden. Drain on paper towels and keep warm while you cook the remaining salmon sticks. Serve with the potato wedges.

Tuna with a Chile Crust

INGREDIENTS

serves 4

1 small bunch fresh cilantro or flat-leaf parsley

3–4 dried red chiles, crushed

2 tbsp sesame seeds

1 egg white

4 tuna steaks, about 5–6 oz/ 140–175 g each

2–3 tbsp corn oil

salt and pepper

lime wedges, to garnish

1 Chop the cilantro, leaving a few leaves whole to garnish. Mix the crushed chiles, chopped cilantro, and sesame seeds together in a shallow dish and season to taste with salt and pepper. Lightly beat the egg white with a fork in a separate shallow dish.

2 Dip the tuna steaks first in the egg white, then in the chile and herb mixture to coat. Gently pat the crust evenly over the fish with the palm of your hand, making sure that both sides of the steaks are well covered.

3 Heat the oil in a large heavy-bottom skillet. Add the tuna and cook over medium heat for 4 minutes, then turn over carefully, using a spatula. Cook for an additional 4 minutes, then transfer to warmed serving plates. Garnish with the lime wedges and the reserved cilantro leaves, and serve immediately.

Spaghetti with Tuna & Parsley

INGREDIENTS

1 lb 2 oz/500 g dried
spaghetti

2 tbsp butter

7 oz/200 g canned tuna,
drained and flaked

2 oz/55 g canned anchovies,
drained

1 cup olive oil

1 cup coarsely chopped
fresh flat-leaf parsley

⅔ cup sour cream

salt and pepper

serves 6

1 Bring a large heavy-bottom pan of lightly salted water to a boil. Add the spaghetti, return to a boil, and cook for 8–10 minutes, or until tender but still firm to the bite. Drain the spaghetti and return to the pan. Add the butter, toss thoroughly to coat, and keep warm until needed.

2 Place the tuna in a food processor or blender with the anchovies, oil, and parsley, and process until the sauce is smooth. Pour in the sour cream and process for a few seconds to blend. Taste the sauce and season with salt and pepper, if necessary.

3 Shake the pan of spaghetti over medium heat for a few minutes, or until it is thoroughly warmed through. Pour the sauce over the spaghetti and toss quickly. Serve immediately.

Broiled Trout

INGREDIENTS

serves ❹

2 tbsp chopped toasted hazelnuts

2 tbsp ground almonds

1 cup grated cheddar cheese

4 tbsp fresh breadcrumbs, white or whole wheat

1 egg

1 tbsp milk

4 brown trout fillets, about 6 oz/175 g each

2 tbsp all-purpose flour

salt and pepper

1 Preheat the broiler to medium. Place the hazelnuts and almonds in a large bowl. Add the cheese and breadcrumbs and mix together. Place the egg and milk in a separate bowl and beat together. Season to taste with salt and pepper.

2 Rinse the fish fillets and pat dry with paper towels. Coat the fillets in the flour, then dip them into the egg mixture. Transfer them to the bowl containing the nuts and cheese, and turn the fillets in the mixture until thoroughly coated.

3 Cook the fish under the preheated broiler for 5 minutes, turning once during the cooking time, or until golden and cooked through. Remove from the broiler and transfer to warmed plates. Serve immediately.

Monkfish Stir-Fry

INGREDIENTS

serves 4

2 tsp sesame oil

1 lb/450 g monkfish fillets, cut into 1-inch/2.5-cm chunks

1 onion, thinly sliced

3 garlic cloves, finely chopped

1 tsp grated fresh ginger

8 oz/225 g fine tip asparagus

3 cups thinly sliced mushrooms

2 tbsp soy sauce

1 tbsp lemon juice

1 Heat the oil in a skillet over medium–high heat. Add the monkfish, onion, garlic, ginger, asparagus, and mushrooms. Stir-fry for 2–3 minutes.

2 Stir in the soy sauce and lemon juice and cook for an additional minute.

3 Remove from the heat and transfer to warmed serving dishes. Serve immediately.

Sea Bass with Fennel Butter

INGREDIENTS

serves **2**

2 small sea bass, about 12 oz/350 g each, scaled, gutted, and heads removed

2 tsp fennel seeds, crushed

3 tbsp all-purpose flour

1 tbsp vegetable oil

½ cup butter

juice of ½ lemon

1 tbsp finely chopped fresh flat-leaf parsley

salt and pepper

lemon wedges, to garnish

1 Slash the sea bass 2–3 times on each side. Stuff half the fennel seeds into the slits. Dredge the fish in the flour.

2 Heat the oil and 2 tablespoons of the butter in a heavy-bottom nonstick skillet over medium–high heat. Cook the fish for 1½ minutes on each side, until browned. Season generously with salt and pepper, and sprinkle over the lemon juice. Reduce the heat to medium, cover the pan, and cook for 5 minutes, then turn and cook for an additional 2–3 minutes, until the flesh is opaque.

3 Transfer the fish to warmed serving plates. Wipe out the pan with paper towels, add the remaining butter and fennel seeds, and cook over medium–high heat until golden and foaming. Pour over the fish, sprinkle with the parsley, and serve immediately, garnished with lemon wedges.

Pan-Fried Halibut Steaks with Tomato Salsa

INGREDIENTS

1 tbsp vegetable oil

4 tbsp butter

4 halibut steaks, about 1 inch/2.5 cm thick

all-purpose flour, for dusting

juice of ½ lemon

salt and pepper

TOMATO SALSA

3 firm tomatoes, halved, seeded, and finely diced

1 small red onion, finely diced

1 green chile, seeded and finely diced

3 tbsp chopped fresh cilantro

juice of 1 lime

½ tsp sea salt

serves ❹

1 Combine all the salsa ingredients in a serving bowl and let stand at room temperature.

2 Heat the oil and 3 tablespoons of the butter in a large skillet over medium–high heat. Dust the halibut steaks with flour and season to taste with salt and pepper. Place in the skillet and cook for 5 minutes on one side and 3–4 minutes on the other, until golden and cooked through. Transfer to a warmed serving dish.

3 Add the lemon juice to the skillet and simmer over medium heat for a few seconds, scraping up any sediment from the bottom of the skillet. Stir in the remaining butter and cook for a few seconds. Pour over the fish and serve immediately with the salsa.

Barbecued Mackerel

INGREDIENTS

4 mackerel

2 tbsp olive oil

2 tbsp lemon juice

sea salt and pepper

lemon wedges and cooked green beans, to serve

serves ❹

1 Clean and gut the fish and remove the heads. Make diagonal slashes on each side of the flesh. Rub all over with the oil, lemon juice, sea salt, and pepper, pushing the salt and pepper well into the slashes.

2 Preheat the barbecue or broiler. Cook the mackerel over hot coals or under the preheated broiler for 5–6 minutes on each side.

3 Transfer to warmed plates and serve with lemon wedges and cooked green beans.

Linguine with Anchovies, Olives & Capers

INGREDIENTS

3 tbsp olive oil

2 garlic cloves, finely chopped

10 anchovy fillets, drained and chopped

scant 1 cup black olives, pitted and chopped

1 tbsp capers, rinsed

1 lb/450 g plum tomatoes, peeled, seeded, and chopped

pinch of cayenne pepper

14 oz/400 g dried linguine

salt

2 tbsp chopped fresh flat-leaf parsley, to garnish

serves 4

1 Heat the oil in a heavy-bottom pan. Add the garlic and cook over low heat, stirring frequently, for 2 minutes. Add the anchovies and mash them to a pulp with a fork. Add the olives, capers, and tomatoes and season to taste with cayenne pepper. Cover and let simmer for 25 minutes.

2 Meanwhile, bring a pan of lightly salted water to a boil. Add the pasta, bring back to a boil, and cook for 8–10 minutes, until tender but still firm to the bite. Drain and transfer to a warmed serving dish.

3 Spoon the anchovy sauce into the dish and toss the pasta, using 2 large forks. Garnish with the parsley and serve immediately.

Shrimp & Lime Kabobs

INGREDIENTS

serves 4

20 raw jumbo shrimp

**1 red onion, cut into
1-inch/2.5-cm chunks**

**½ yellow and ½ red bell
pepper, seeded and cut into
1-inch/2.5-cm chunks**

lime wedges, to garnish

**cooked rice and lime and
ginger chutney, to serve**

MARINADE

⅓ cup lime juice

finely grated rind of 1 lime

2 tbsp olive oil

1 garlic clove, crushed

**1 green chile, seeded and
thinly sliced**

**2 tsp finely chopped fresh
flat-leaf parsley**

salt and pepper

1 Peel the shrimp, leaving the tails intact. Cut a slot along the back of each shrimp, then remove and discard the dark vein.

2 Place the marinade ingredients in a screw-top jar and shake well. Place the shrimp in a shallow dish and the onion and bell pepper chunks in a separate dish. Divide the marinade between the two dishes, tossing the shrimp and vegetables to coat. Cover and let chill in the refrigerator for at least 1 hour.

3 Preheat the barbecue or broiler. Thread the ingredients onto four metal or presoaked wooden skewers, alternating the shrimp and vegetables. Cook over hot coals or under the preheated broiler for 10 minutes, turning occasionally. Garnish with lime wedges and serve with cooked rice and chutney.

Mussel & Potato Gratin

INGREDIENTS

serves **4**

1 lb 5oz/600 g live mussels,
scrubbed and debearded

1 large onion, thinly sliced

14 oz/400 g canned chopped
tomatoes

1 lb/450 g new potatoes,
thinly sliced

3 tbsp chopped fresh
flat-leaf parsley

2 garlic cloves, finely
chopped

scant 1 cup coarsely grated
pecorino cheese

olive oil, for drizzling

scant 1 cup coarse stale
breadcrumbs

salt and pepper

1 Discard any mussels with broken shells or any that refuse to close when tapped. Place in a saucepan with 1 cup of water and cook, covered, over high heat for 3–4 minutes. Strain through a cheesecloth-lined strainer, reserving the liquid. Discard any mussels that remain closed. Discard one half of each shell, and set aside the other half-shell containing the flesh.

2 Preheat the oven to 350°F/180°C. Spread half the onion over the bottom of a 2 quart/2 liter baking dish. Add half the tomatoes and half the potatoes, then repeat the layers with the remaining onion, tomatoes, and potatoes, sprinkling with the parsley and garlic, and seasoning well with salt and pepper. Top with one-third of the pecorino cheese. Pour over 1 cup of the mussel liquid and drizzle with oil.

3 Bake in the preheated oven for 40 minutes. Arrange the reserved mussels in their half-shells on top and sprinkle with the remaining cheese and the breadcrumbs. Increase the heat to 400°F/200°C and bake for an additional 10 minutes, until golden. Serve immediately.

Seared Scallops & Leeks

INGREDIENTS

4 thin leeks, halved lengthwise then crosswise

5 tbsp olive oil

20 large scallops

sea salt and pepper

snipped fresh chives and lemon wedges, to garnish

serves 4

1 Preheat the oven to 450°F/230°C. Arrange the leeks cut-side up in a single layer in an ovenproof dish. Drizzle with 3 tablespoons of the oil, then sprinkle with sea salt and pepper, pushing it into the crevices. Bake in the preheated oven for 8–10 minutes, until browned at the edges but still bright green and tender-crisp.

2 Score the scallops with crisscross slashes. Heat the remaining oil in a skillet over high heat. Cook the scallops for 3–4 minutes, until just browned but slightly translucent on the inside.

3 Remove the leeks from the oven and arrange on warmed serving plates with the scallops on top. Simmer the scallop juices in the pan until slightly reduced, then pour over the scallops and leeks. Garnish with chives and lemon wedges, and serve immediately.

5 Vegetarian

Vegetarian meals are perfect for exploring the sheer variety of dishes that can be cooked in only three steps. By combining pantry ingredients with top-notch fresh vegetables, cheese, or eggs, you can have colorful, flavor-packed dishes on the table in very little time at all. Many of the dishes in this chapter can be prepared ahead and reheated when you need them—perfect for a speedy supper or a lunch on the run.

Mushroom Stroganoff

INGREDIENTS

2 tbsp butter

1 onion, finely chopped

1 lb/450 g button
mushrooms, quartered

1 tsp tomato paste

1 tsp coarse-grain mustard

⅔ cup sour cream

1 tsp paprika, plus extra
to garnish

salt and pepper

fresh flat-leaf parsley
sprigs, to garnish

serves ❹

1 Heat the butter in a large heavy-bottom skillet. Add the onion and cook gently for 5–10 minutes, until softened.

2 Add the mushrooms to the skillet and stir-fry for a few minutes, until they start to soften. Stir in the tomato paste and mustard, then add the sour cream. Cook gently, stirring constantly, for 5 minutes.

3 Stir in the paprika and season to taste with salt and pepper. Garnish with paprika and parsley sprigs, and serve immediately.

Bean & Vegetable Chili

INGREDIENTS

4 tbsp vegetable stock

1 onion, coarsely chopped

1 green bell pepper, seeded and finely chopped

1 red bell pepper, seeded and finely chopped

1 tsp finely chopped garlic

1 tsp finely chopped fresh ginger

2 tsp ground cumin

½ tsp chili powder

2 tbsp tomato paste

14 oz/400 g canned chopped tomatoes

14 oz/400 g canned kidney beans, drained

14 oz/400 g canned black-eyed peas, drained

salt and pepper

corn tortillas, to serve

serves 4

1 Heat the stock in a large saucepan, add the onion and bell peppers, and simmer for 5 minutes, or until softened.

2 Stir in the garlic, ginger, cumin, chili powder, tomato paste, and tomatoes. Season to taste with salt and pepper, and simmer for 10 minutes.

3 Stir in the kidney beans and black-eyed peas and simmer for an additional 5 minutes, or until hot. Remove the pan from the heat and transfer the chili to a warmed serving dish. Serve with corn tortillas.

Linguine with Wild Mushroom & Mascarpone Sauce

INGREDIENTS

1 lb/450 g dried linguine

4 tbsp butter

1 garlic clove, crushed

8 oz/225 g mixed wild mushrooms

heaping 1 cup mascarpone cheese

2 tbsp milk

1 tsp chopped fresh sage, plus extra leaves to garnish

salt and pepper

Parmesan cheese shavings, to serve

serves 4

1 Bring a large heavy-bottom saucepan of lightly salted water to a boil. Add the pasta, return to a boil, and cook for 8–10 minutes, until tender but still firm to the bite.

2 Meanwhile, melt the butter in a separate large pan. Add the garlic and mushrooms and cook for 3–4 minutes. Reduce the heat and stir in the mascarpone cheese, milk, and chopped sage. Season to taste with salt and pepper.

3 Drain the pasta thoroughly and add to the mushroom sauce. Toss until the pasta is well coated with the sauce. Transfer to warmed dishes, garnish with sage leaves, and serve immediately with Parmesan cheese shavings.

Pasta with Basil & Pine Nut Pesto

INGREDIENTS

serves **4**

about 40 fresh basil leaves

3 garlic cloves, crushed

2 tbsp pine nuts

scant ½ cup finely grated
Parmesan cheese, plus
extra to serve

2–3 tbsp extra virgin olive oil

12 oz/350 g dried pasta

salt and pepper

1 Rinse the basil leaves and pat them dry with paper towels. Place the basil leaves, garlic, pine nuts, and Parmesan cheese in a food processor and blend for 30 seconds, or until smooth. With the motor running, slowly add enough of the oil to reach the desired consistency. Season to taste with salt and pepper.

2 Bring a large heavy-bottom saucepan of lightly salted water to a boil. Add the pasta, return to a boil, and cook for 8–10 minutes, until tender but still firm to the bite.

3 Drain the pasta thoroughly, then transfer to a serving plate and add the pesto. Toss well to mix and serve with extra grated Parmesan cheese.

Creamy Spinach & Mushroom Pasta

INGREDIENTS

10½ oz/300 g dried pasta

2 tbsp olive oil

9 oz/250 g mushrooms, sliced

1 tsp dried oregano

scant 1¼ cups vegetable stock

1 tbsp lemon juice

6 tbsp cream cheese

1 cup frozen spinach leaves

salt and pepper

serves 4

1 Bring a large heavy-bottom saucepan of lightly salted water to a boil. Add the pasta, return to a boil, and cook for 8–10 minutes, until tender but still firm to the bite. Drain, reserving ¾ cup of the cooking liquid.

2 Meanwhile, heat the oil in a large heavy-bottom skillet over medium heat, add the mushrooms, and cook, stirring frequently, for 8 minutes, or until almost crisp. Stir in the oregano, stock, and lemon juice and cook for 10–12 minutes, or until the sauce is reduced by half.

3 Stir in the cream cheese and spinach and cook over medium–low heat for 3–5 minutes. Add the reserved cooking liquid, then the cooked pasta. Stir well, season to taste with salt and pepper, and heat through before serving.

Red Onion & Goat Cheese Tartlets

INGREDIENTS

2 tbsp olive oil

4 red onions, halved and thinly sliced

2 tbsp balsamic vinegar

2 tbsp stock

1 tsp sugar

1 tsp fresh thyme leaves

7 oz/200 g prepared short crust pie dough

2 tbsp pine nuts

4 thin slices goat cheese from a log

salt and pepper

serves ❹

1 Preheat the oven to 350°F/180°C. Heat the oil in large heavy-bottom skillet over medium heat. Add the onions and cook gently for 15 minutes, stirring frequently. Stir in the vinegar, stock, sugar, and thyme. Season to taste with salt and pepper. Cook, stirring, for an additional 20 minutes.

2 Meanwhile, roll out the pie dough and use to line four 4½-inch/12-cm tartlet pans. Line with foil and fill with pie weights or dried beans. Bake in the preheated oven for 10 minutes. Remove the foil and pie weights.

3 Spread the onion mixture over the bottoms of the pastry shells. Sprinkle with the pine nuts and arrange the goat cheese on top. Bake for 15 minutes, until the cheese is melted and starting to color. Serve hot.

Baked Sweet Potatoes with Ginger & Cilantro

INGREDIENTS

4 sweet potatoes, about
10½ oz/300 g each

vegetable oil, for brushing

4 tbsp butter

1½ oz/40 g fresh ginger,
sliced into very thin
matchsticks

2 tbsp chopped fresh
cilantro

salt and pepper

serves ❹

1 Preheat the oven to 450°F/230°C. Brush
the sweet potatoes with oil and bake in the
preheated oven for 40–45 minutes, until tender.
Cut a cross in the top of each potato. Press the
flesh upward until it bursts through the cuts.

2 Heat the butter in a skillet over medium–high
heat, until foaming. Add the ginger and cook
for 3–4 minutes, until golden and crisp.

3 Pour the ginger and buttery juices over the
potatoes. Sprinkle with the cilantro, season to
taste with salt and pepper, and serve

Snow Pea, Sesame & Bean Curd Stir-Fry

INGREDIENTS

serves 2 to 3

2 tbsp toasted sesame oil

3 tbsp peanut oil

7 oz/200 g small shiitake mushrooms

2 heads bok choy, leaves left whole, stalks sliced

5 oz/150 g snow peas, sliced in half at an angle

9-oz/250-g package bean curd, drained and cubed

1¼-inch/3-cm piece fresh ginger, thinly sliced

2 garlic cloves, finely chopped

1 tbsp soy sauce

1 tsp sesame seeds

salt and pepper

cooked noodles, to serve

1 Heat the two oils in a wok over high heat. Add the mushrooms, bok choy stalks, and snow peas, and stir-fry for 1 minute.

2 Add the bean curd, bok choy leaves, ginger, garlic, and a splash of water to moisten. Stir-fry for an additional 1–2 minutes, until the bok choy leaves have wilted.

3 Stir in the soy sauce, sprinkle with the sesame seeds, and season to taste with salt and pepper. Serve immediately with cooked noodles.

Baked Bell Peppers with Olives & Feta

INGREDIENTS

4 bell peppers, red and yellow, halved and seeded

3 garlic cloves, crushed

1 tsp finely chopped fresh rosemary

1 tsp fresh thyme leaves

¾ cup coarse stale breadcrumbs

3 tbsp extra virgin olive oil

7 black olives, pitted

50 g/2 oz feta cheese, cut into ½-inch/1-cm cubes

salt and pepper

serves 2

1 Preheat the oven to 475°F/240°C. Place the bell peppers cut-side down in a shallow roasting pan. Bake in the preheated oven for 20 minutes, until the skin wrinkles and begins to blacken. Remove the pan from the oven, cover with a thick dish towel, and let stand for 5 minutes, then peel the skin off the bell peppers.

2 Reduce the oven temperature to 425°F/220°C. Cut the bell peppers into bite-size chunks and place in a shallow ovenproof dish. Combine the garlic, herbs, and breadcrumbs in a small bowl. Season to taste with salt and pepper, and stir in the oil. Scatter the mixture over the bell peppers and top with the olives and feta cheese.

3 Bake in the preheated oven for 10–15 minutes, until the breadcrumbs are crisp and the cheese is starting to color.

Braised Borlotti Beans & Tomatoes with Parmesan Toasts

INGREDIENTS

serves 4

7 tbsp olive oil

10–12 fresh sage leaves, coarsely chopped

1 red onion, thinly sliced

2 large garlic cloves, thinly sliced

14 oz/400 g canned chopped tomatoes

1 tbsp tomato paste

1 lb 12 oz/800 g canned borlotti beans, drained and rinsed

8 thin slices ciabatta bread

½ cup freshly grated Parmesan cheese

salt and pepper

1 Heat 5 tablespoons of the oil in a large heavy-bottom saucepan over medium heat. Add the sage, onion, and garlic and cook gently for 5 minutes. Stir in the tomatoes and tomato paste, and cook for an additional 2–3 minutes, stirring.

2 Add the beans, cover, and cook for 20 minutes, adding a little water or stock if necessary—the mixture should be soupy. Season to taste with salt and pepper.

3 Preheat the broiler to medium. Drizzle the remaining oil over the bread and sprinkle with the Parmesan cheese. Place under a preheated broiler for a few minutes, until the cheese is golden and bubbling. Divide the slices of toasted bread among 4 warmed serving dishes and spoon the bean mixture over the top. Serve immediately.

Spicy Fried Eggs

INGREDIENTS

2 tbsp olive oil

1 large onion, finely chopped

2 green or red bell peppers, seeded and coarsely chopped

1 garlic clove, finely chopped

½ tsp dried chile flakes

4 plum tomatoes, peeled and coarsely chopped

2 eggs

1 tbsp chopped fresh flat-leaf parsley

salt and pepper

serves ❷

1 Heat the oil in a large nonstick skillet over medium heat. Add the onion and cook until golden. Add the bell peppers, garlic, and chile flakes, and cook until the bell peppers are softened.

2 Stir in the tomatoes, season to taste with salt and pepper, and simmer over medium–low heat for 10 minutes.

3 Using the back of a spoon, make 2 depressions in the mixture in the skillet. Break the eggs into the depressions, cover, and cook for 3–4 minutes, until the eggs are set. Sprinkle with the parsley and serve.

French Lentils Provençal

INGREDIENTS

serves ❷

2 tbsp olive oil

1 zucchini, quartered lengthwise and diced

1 red bell pepper, seeded and diced

2 garlic cloves, crushed

5 oz/150 g cherry tomatoes

14 oz/400 g canned French lentils, drained

1 tsp red wine vinegar

pinch of dried chile flakes

salt and pepper

1 Heat the oil in a heavy-bottom skillet over medium heat. Add the zucchini, bell pepper, and garlic, and cook for 5 minutes, until softened.

2 Add the tomatoes and crush with the back of a wooden spoon. Cook for an additional 1–2 minutes.

3 Stir in the lentils and cook for 3–4 minutes to heat through. Add the vinegar and chile flakes, season to taste with salt and pepper, and serve hot.

Spicy Chickpea & Eggplant Casserole

INGREDIENTS

serves 6

1 tbsp cumin seeds

2 tbsp coriander seeds

2 tsp dried oregano or thyme

5 tbsp vegetable oil

2 onions, chopped

1 red bell pepper, seeded and cut into ¾-inch/2-cm chunks

1 eggplant, cut into ¾-inch/2-cm chunks

2 garlic cloves, chopped

1 green chile, chopped

14 oz/400 g canned chopped tomatoes

14 oz/400 g canned chickpeas, drained and rinsed

8 oz/225 g green beans, cut into ¾-inch/2-cm lengths

2½ cups stock

3 tbsp chopped fresh cilantro

1 Dry-roast the seeds in a heavy-bottom skillet for a few seconds, until aromatic. Add the oregano and cook for an additional few seconds. Remove from the heat, transfer to a mortar, and crush with a pestle.

2 Heat the oil in a large flameproof casserole dish. Cook the onions, bell pepper, and eggplant for 10 minutes, until softened. Add the ground seed mixture, garlic, and chile, and cook for an additional 2 minutes.

3 Add the tomatoes, chickpeas, green beans, and stock. Bring to a boil, then cover and simmer gently for 1 hour. Stir in the cilantro and serve immediately.

5 Sweet Treats

Desserts are a treat but we often don't have the time to make them. The recipes here show you that three steps are all it takes to concoct a creamy tiramisu or crème brûlée, a fragrant fruit compote, or an irresistible cheesecake. There are also no-fuss recipes for oat bars, gingerbread, and chocolate chip cookies—delicious snacks to have on hand when you're in the mood for something sweet.

Creamy Rice Pudding

INGREDIENTS

1 tbsp butter, for greasing

½ cup golden raisins, plus extra to decorate

5 tbsp superfine sugar

3¼ oz/90 g sweet rice

5 cups milk

1 tsp vanilla extract

finely grated rind of 1 large lemon

pinch of nutmeg

chopped pistachios, to decorate

serves 4

1 Preheat the oven to 325°F/160°C. Grease a 3½-cup/850-ml ovenproof dish with butter.

2 Put the golden raisins, sugar, and rice into a mixing bowl, then stir in the milk and vanilla extract. Transfer to the prepared dish, sprinkle over the grated lemon rind and the nutmeg, then bake in the preheated oven for 2½ hours.

3 Remove from the oven and transfer to individual serving bowls. Decorate with golden raisins and chopped pistachios and serve.

Cheat's Crème Brûlée

INGREDIENTS

serves ❹ to ❻

scant 1½ cups mixed berries, such as blueberries, strawberries, and raspberries

1½–2 tbsp Cointreau or orange flower water

1⅛ cups mascarpone cheese

scant 1 cup sour cream

2–3 tbsp brown sugar

1 Prepare the fruit, if necessary, and lightly rinse, then place in the bottoms of 4–6 x ⅔-cup/ 150-ml ramekins. Sprinkle the fruit with the Cointreau.

2 Cream the mascarpone cheese in a bowl until soft, then gradually beat in the sour cream. Spoon the mascarpone mixture over the fruit, smoothing the surface and ensuring that the tops are level. Let chill in the refrigerator for at least 2 hours.

3 Sprinkle the tops with the sugar. Using a chef's blowtorch, broil the tops until caramelized, about 2–3 minutes. Alternatively, cook under a preheated broiler, turning the dishes, for 3–4 minutes, or until the tops are lightly caramelized all over. Serve immediately or let chill in the refrigerator for 15–20 minutes before serving.

Chocolate Mousse

INGREDIENTS

10½ oz/300 g semisweet chocolate

1½ tbsp unsalted butter

1 tbsp brandy

4 eggs, separated

serves ❹

1 Break the chocolate into small pieces and place in a heatproof bowl set over a pan of gently simmering water. Add the butter and melt with the chocolate, stirring, until smooth. Remove from the heat, stir in the brandy, and let cool slightly. Add the egg yolks and beat until smooth.

2 In a separate bowl, whisk the egg whites until stiff peaks have formed, then fold them into the chocolate mixture. Spoon the mixture into 4 small serving bowls and level the surfaces. Transfer to the refrigerator and chill for at least 4 hours, until set.

3 Take the mousse out of the refrigerator and serve.

Tiramisu

INGREDIENTS

1 cup strong black coffee, cooled to room temperature

4 tbsp orange liqueur, such as Cointreau

3 tbsp orange juice

16 Italian ladyfingers

heaping 1 cup mascarpone cheese

1¼ cups heavy cream, lightly whipped

3 tbsp confectioners' sugar

grated rind of 1 orange

2¼ oz/60 g semisweet chocolate, grated

chopped toasted almonds and strips of orange zest, to decorate

serves ❹

1 Pour the cooled coffee into a pitcher and stir in the orange liqueur and orange juice. Place 8 of the ladyfingers in the bottom of a serving dish, then pour over half of the coffee mixture.

2 Place the mascarpone cheese in a separate bowl together with the cream, confectioners' sugar, and orange rind and mix well. Spread half of the mascarpone mixture over the coffee-soaked ladyfingers, then arrange the remaining ladyfingers on top. Pour over the remaining coffee mixture, then spread over the remaining mascarpone mixture.

3 Sprinkle over the grated chocolate and chill in the refrigerator for at least 2 hours. Serve decorated with chopped toasted almonds and strips of orange zest.

Deep Chocolate Cheesecake

INGREDIENTS

serves **4** to **6**

4 oz/115 g graham crackers, finely crushed

2 tsp unsweetened cocoa

4 tbsp butter, melted, plus extra for greasing

chocolate leaves, to decorate

CHOCOLATE LAYER

1 lb 12 oz/800 g mascarpone cheese

scant 2 cups confectioners' sugar, sifted

juice of ½ orange

finely grated rind of 1 orange

6 oz/175 g semisweet chocolate, melted

2 tbsp brandy

1 Grease an 8-inch/20-cm loose-bottom cake pan. To make the base, put the crushed graham crackers, cocoa, and melted butter into a large bowl and mix well. Press the crumb mixture evenly over the bottom of the prepared pan.

2 Put the mascarpone cheese and confectioners' sugar into a bowl and stir in the orange juice and orange rind. Add the melted chocolate and brandy, and mix together until thoroughly combined. Spread the chocolate mixture evenly over the crumb layer. Cover with plastic wrap and let chill for at least 4 hours.

3 Remove the cheesecake from the refrigerator, turn out onto a serving platter, and decorate with chocolate leaves. Serve immediately.

Apple Strudel with Warm Cider Sauce

INGREDIENTS

serves **2** to **4**

8 apples

1 tbsp lemon juice

½ cup golden raisins

1 tsp ground cinnamon

½ tsp grated nutmeg

1 tbsp light brown sugar

6 sheets filo dough

vegetable oil spray

confectioners' sugar, for dusting

CIDER SAUCE

1 tbsp cornstarch

2 cups hard cider

1 Preheat the oven to 375°F/190°C. Line a baking sheet with parchment paper. Peel and core the apples and chop them into ½-inch/ 1-cm cubes. Toss the pieces in a bowl with the lemon juice, golden raisins, cinnamon, nutmeg, and brown sugar.

2 Lay out a sheet of filo dough, spray with vegetable oil, and lay a second sheet on top. Repeat with a third sheet. Spread over half the apple mixture and roll up lengthwise, tucking in the ends to enclose the filling. Repeat to make a second strudel. Slide onto the baking sheet, spray with oil, and bake in the preheated oven for 15–20 minutes.

3 For the sauce, blend the cornstarch in a pan with a little hard cider until smooth. Add the remaining hard cider and heat gently, stirring constantly, until the mixture boils and thickens. Serve the strudel warm or cold, dusted with confectioners' sugar, and accompanied by the sauce.

Dark Plum Compote

INGREDIENTS

1 lb 5 oz/600 g dark-skinned plums, halved and pitted

lightly whipped cream, to serve

SYRUP

¾ cup sugar

1¾ cups water

3 fresh bay leaves, torn

1 thinly pared strip of orange zest

serves **4**

1 Place the plum halves in a serving bowl.

2 Place the syrup ingredients in a saucepan. Stir over medium heat until the sugar has dissolved, then boil for 7–10 minutes, until syrupy. Immediately strain the boiling syrup over the plums. Let cool to room temperature.

3 Serve the plum compote with lightly whipped cream.

Basil-Scented Strawberries & Nectarines

INGREDIENTS

1 lb 2 oz/500 g strawberries, hulled

1 tbsp lemon juice

2 ripe nectarines, halved and pitted

10–12 basil leaves, torn

2 tbsp sugar

serves 4

1 Slice the strawberries, if they are large, and place in a bowl with the lemon juice.

2 Slice each of the nectarine halves lengthwise into three segments. Slice each segment in half crosswise and add to the bowl.

3 Crush the basil with the sugar using a mortar and pestle. Add to the fruit and mix well. Let stand for 30 minutes. Serve at room temperature.

Gingerbread Squares

INGREDIENTS

makes **2** **4**

7 tbsp butter, plus extra
for greasing

generous ¼ cup packed
brown sugar

5 tbsp molasses

1 egg white

1 tsp almond extract

scant 1¼ cups all-purpose
flour, plus extra for dusting

¼ tsp baking soda

¼ tsp baking powder

pinch of salt

½ tsp allspice

½ tsp ground ginger

4½ oz/125 g apples, cooked
and finely chopped

1 Preheat the oven to 350°F/180°C. Grease a large baking sheet and line it with parchment paper. Put the butter, sugar, molasses, egg white, and almond extract into a food processor and blend until smooth.

2 In a separate bowl, sift the flour, baking soda, baking powder, salt, allspice, and ginger together. Add to the creamed mixture and beat together thoroughly. Stir in the chopped apples. Pour the mixture onto the prepared baking sheet.

3 Transfer to the preheated oven and bake for 10 minutes, or until golden brown. Remove from the oven and cut into 24 pieces. Transfer the squares to a wire rack and let them cool completely before serving.

Chocolate Chip Cookies

INGREDIENTS

1½ cups all-purpose flour, sifted

1 tsp baking powder

½ cup soft margarine, plus extra for greasing

scant ⅔ cup light brown sugar

¼ cup superfine sugar

½ tsp vanilla extract

1 egg

⅔ cup semisweet chocolate chips

makes 18

1 Preheat the oven to 375°F/190°C. Place all the ingredients in a large mixing bowl and beat until they are thoroughly combined.

2 Lightly grease 2 baking sheets. Place 9 tablespoonfuls of the mixture onto each baking sheet, spacing them well apart to allow for spreading during cooking.

3 Bake in the preheated oven for 10–12 minutes, until the cookies are golden brown. Using a spatula, transfer the cookies to a cooling rack to cool completely before serving.

Nutty Oat Bars

INGREDIENTS

scant 2¾ cups rolled oats

¾ cup chopped hazelnuts

6 tbsp all-purpose flour

½ cup butter, plus extra for greasing

2 tbsp dark corn syrup

scant ½ cup light brown sugar

makes ❶❻

1 Preheat the oven to 350°F/180°C, then grease a 9-inch/23-cm square cake pan. Place the rolled oats, chopped hazelnuts, and flour in a large mixing bowl and stir together.

2 Place the butter, corn syrup, and sugar in a pan over low heat and stir until melted. Pour onto the dry ingredients and mix well. Turn into the prepared cake pan and smooth the surface with the back of a spoon.

3 Bake in the preheated oven for 20–25 minutes, or until golden and firm to the touch. Mark into 16 pieces and let cool in the pan. When completely cooled, cut through with a sharp knife and remove from the pan.

Marshmallow Float

INGREDIENTS

8 oz/225 g semisweet chocolate, broken into pieces

3¾ cups milk

3 tbsp superfine sugar

8 marshmallows

serves ❹

1 Finely chop the chocolate with a knife or in a food processor. Do not overprocess or the chocolate will melt.

2 Pour the milk into a pan and bring to just below boiling point. Remove the pan from the heat and whisk in the sugar and the chocolate.

3 Pour into heatproof glasses, top each with two marshmallows, and serve immediately.

Index